Dedication..............................3
The Meditational Prayer................4
This is Why I Write..................6
Blood Stain......................7-9
Straight Genes/Loose Jeans..........10-12
(Free Verse)...........................13
Soul Ties.........................14-15
Insanity (Dedicated to JUW)..............16-17
(Free Verse)..............................18
Junkie Gene (Dedicated to LS)................19-21
Crowns..............................22-24
Jewel Box............................25-26
(Free Verse)...........................27
Immigrant Mentality.......................28-30
The Body of this Essay Prose......................31
(Free Verse)..............................32
(Free Verse)..............................33
The Bride & Groom.........................34-35
MasterPeace..............................36-37
***Sphinx of Giza**............................38*
(Free Verse)..............................39
Legacy..............................40
(Free Verse)..............................41
Acknowledgements............................42
About the Author...........................43

Dedication

UnCover'd Vol. 1, an original collection of poetry, is dedicated to all the creative free thinkers of their generation. *UnCover'd Vol.1* is a raw celebration of victory for those who are willing to become unstoppable in their purpose. This small volume is written to remind us to treat everyone with kindness and mercy, because we never know the internal battle it takes for another to survive. I hope these pages reach you in which ever season your hands grace the pages.

Sherrie Elle poetry

Meditational Prayer
(5/2007) (4/13/2018)

Father God, Mother Nature and the Universe:
I ask that you weigh the actions of the heart,
And rescue this world
From the destruction that has divided us apart.
I also ask that you shed your mercy
On those who try to curse me.
As we may be under an attack,
Please help us to remember one fact:
That this life is chosen as a celebration
And not a means of competition,
So sharpen us daily with our own personal mission.

Let us keep our mind on righteousness;
Not on temporary ideas of bliss,
For this way is a death risk
That we should not take
For the sake
Of all beings and creatures alike.
Because harmony must live within
And not in hatred, cruelty or spite.
Give us all understanding of Higher expectations,
For knowledge of this will help our every relation.
Why be conformed to this box we call Earth,
And this limited existence
While there are beings beyond this planet finite dimension.
So why not transform the mind
Let's allow our thoughts to be concentrated on Love, Truth,
Justice and Balance

Because an unstable collective can never be honest.
So instead of the limits of religion and doctrine, and ethnicity

Allow human kind to be spiritual fruit that will constantly
grow,
Because our actions produce a harvest that we will reap what
we sow.

I have faith that beauty lies in creation
Because destruction will never last
So, let's devote our time,
Energy;
Life force
And soul,
To our Higher calling,
Because in this crazy world,
Use kindness as the most powerful sword.

This Is Why I Write
(2001) (2017)

I can't really share
what I been through in fear
Of being shamed away;
So, I just wipe the tears hoping to wipe the pain away.
I know there's people who feel the same way,
But at times it feels as if the rain won't go away.
Because for so long,
The battles with dreariness,
And weariness,
Of a heart that is far from broken;
Times where I've spoken
up--
To just be brought down again,
By a friend,
Who thought they could judge or understand me to the end.

But I write because it's me;
Without writing I'd be stripped of an identity.
So, I write all the time,
With endless rhymes;
Only until I can't do it anymore
And once my hands get cramp and sore,
And
My brain won't allow me to think,
I'll wait--
Another year will pass,
More challenges won't persevere or last.
There'll be enough ink in pens,
Fake people will pose as friends,
to allow me to write again,
Just enough for me to fight to win.

Blood Stain
(4/17/2018)

There are some bruises that you will never forget;
While other scars remain on your heart,
Engraved with regret.
It's that first black eye, *'boo boo'*[1] and blemish mark that
causes the most pain,
But how do you remove a blood stain?
The spot you let soak into your clothes and penetrate through
every fiber;
Not one Band-Aid, or medication a doctor would prescribe
you,
Could treat it.
So that injury becomes infected--
With your mistreatment.
But,
I still don't know how to get the blood out of my favorite shirt,
those familiar pants,
Or that one special skirt;
Kind of ironic because I can recall the first hurt.

Yes, I tried
Every chemical solution:
Detergent Gain, Clorox bleach, and Tide;
Mixed with baking soda and peroxide,
But the stain was never removed;
In fact, the spot only spread and quickly moved.
So,
I threw all those clothes away--
Went out and bought a fancier blouse, no skirts, but prettier
dresses,
Yet, it was still something about me that was so unimpressive.

---

[1] *'boo boo-a slang term to describe a minor injury such as a scratch*

Because those elaborate patterns,
And accessories
That became a work of art,
Only hid an infectious sore--
A virus deep within my heart.
It's interesting how we go through life as if stains on our clothes are worse than a corrupt mind and bloody hands?
As a result, we never become fully clean and issues only expand.
We put Band-Aids over man-made bruises,
As our Higher calling urges us to shift when feel we can't do this.
But we put on another name brand, a different outfit;
Choose another lifestyle tailored to our likings,
As we never realize hidden demons we continue to fight,
And for those who are too *'uppity'*[2], and
What some like to call *"high sadity"*[3];
God frowns on that,
But respect is found in humility with an ounce of dignity.
So be careful whose faces we drag through the mud;
Because if the rain comes down on our house,
The roof would do more than overflood.

So, let the blood stains remain,
Because new clothes,
Won't cover up damages and holes
That tend to infect the unconscious soul.
Bleach and detergent can wash away signs of a war battle,
But once the stain is revealed, it can longer live comfortably in the shadows.

---

[2] *Uppity-an informal term for arrogant or proud*

[3] *Sadity-slang adjective for conceited; "stuck up"*

Straight Genes/Loose Jeans
(5/13/2018)

Some argue that it's in the genes,
And that may be true;
Others say it's in one's personality —
"some people just don't care who they screw,"
But I wonder what it is that people see in you?
Tupac said,
*"…it's time to heal our women,
Be real to our women,
And if we don't
We'll have a race of babies
That hate the ladies
That make the babies…"*
But what happens when there isn't a generation of ladies?
And I'm not speaking about female body parts —
I'm talking about a group of women that lack class;
The type that will curse you out in public,
And completely show their sass;
Those that show up half-naked to teacher conferences and wonder why their sons didn't pass.
But like Tupac said,
"I ain't mad at ya."
But let me tell you who will be —
Your sons,
Because those are the ones
That you either call your own,
Or ignore and disown;
Then we wonder why some old men still
Have never grown.
In the early 2000's we got rid of the trend of baggy, loose fit denim,
And now the guys wear slim fit,
Or skinny jeans —
Barely enough to fit anything in the pockets;
Maybe a phone,

A wallet;
Some even carry a purse or hide make-up palettes.

As people, we are naturally drawn to where we're celebrated
And not just tolerated.
So if he's "too sweet" to play sports;
Not skilled enough to dribble a ball up and down a court,
He's immediately considered "weirdo", "corny", or a "dork".
But no one's listening,
Because we've confined men into these limited boxes,
Asking questions like, *"Do your prefer briefs or boxers?"*
So they easily size women up with brief encounters.

But, what's in your genes?

I've always heard older women say,
*"if you lay down with dogs,
you're bound to get up with fleas."*
They're the ones who teach
Manners like "thank you" and "please",
But these *cougars*[4]
bite like pit bulls,
Then wonder why they don't get treated like ladies.

Who taught men how to gossip?
How does a boy become a *"ladies man"*?
And most importantly,
Why isn't there a term like *"daddy's boy"*?
What's the missing link in that equation?
I promise it'll solve root problems in your most basic relations.
Women can kill with actions or sour words,
Leaving men bitter with tension that remains unheard.

---

[4] *Cougar- An older, experienced woman who finds herself in a sexual or romantic relationships with younger men.*

But it's not the ladies' fault as a whole,
Men there's no excuse for not taking your role.
Deadbeat Father's Day presents expire
Once you don't make parole.
Don't let another man step up to the plate.
Because your child will see your absence
As a dead weight.
And if the person of your dreams stands in the way of the relationship you have with your child —
Then question if the honeymoon stage is truly worth the while.

Mothers give your sons nurturing and care,
By not making him feel like
He must compete with your lover,
Or he can risk the chance of struggling with his identity undercover.
And those mama's boys — the ones we love to "spoil"
With gifts they don't deserve,
Are the ones that can sweet talk any female;
from a size 2, to those with thick curves.

Yet, we spend much more energy shopping for perfect fit jeans for the first date,
But not enough time choosing the right mate,
Then our children suffer the consequences
That were never supposed to be their fate.

Because any person that can honor covenant between child and parent,
Will love God first and that will be clear and apparent.

I don't care how you wear your denim,
Whether baggy, loose fit,
Distressed or shabby;
I'll always appreciate a quality pair of genes--

And so does God,
Just keep your hearts pure and clean.

Shalom.

Free Verse

What you know about others,
Never choose to expose,
Because by the time news reach someone else,
Characters all have the ability to switch roles.
The truth is sacred and we should easily admit,
But a Higher Power is the only judge able to acquit.

2018

Sherrie Elle poetry

Soul Ties
(6/5/2016)

♫ *"There's always that one person that will always have your heart…*
You never see it coming 'cause you're blinded from the start…" ♫
From the start…
Until the very end
I know ♫ *"… he's just a friend"* ♫,
But how did he become more?
The style
The *swag*[5],
His smile, you grew to adore.
Been there time and time before;
Lying to myself but coming back for more.
So, while he kept looking to 'score',
My heart began to explore
All the possibilities--
But, temporary satisfaction was the only open door.
♫ *"…know that you're the one for me,*
It's clear for everyone to see…" ♫
That I was unequally matched
With someone that could never believe in the best version of me—
Yet as a woman, who doesn't enjoy kindness and chivalry?
Higher conscious persisted and yanked at my sleeve,
But this guy seemed to ease every pain that I ever conceived.
Until he
♫ *"…broke my heart* ♫
And I wanted him to
♫ *"…say you love me again"* ♫
But I cried those tears
As my soul wandered.

---

[5] ***Swag-*** *The new generation originally used swag to describe anyone thought to carry themselves in a way considered by some to be sexy / cool.*

Until I thought I erased him,
But I still had his stench,
So I kept turning to men
With the same qualities as this character from back then.
Silent tears and open wounds that didn't seem to heal,
Because new relationships only reopened and revealed
Hurt and pain I thought I escaped.
Now, I realized that hard shell I built was a fake;
It only shattered and crumbled,
Leaving me battered so I stumbled.
When you love so much until it drains and hurt,
What can possibly be worse--
Being blinded by "love",
Or gifted with a curse?
What can a woman do--
Turn to a Higher Source,
But most importantly return to 'you',
Because you are raw metal that goes through the fire to be refined;
A precious stone that has always meant to shine.
The woman, is iron so why rub against a brick--
We then become dull;
God can't use that us a power switch.
And yes,
♪ "...love is blind, and it'll take over your mind, but what you think is love, is truly not, you need to elevate and find..." ♪
So, as you replenish and restore,
Opportunities for growth and fruitful love
Will flourish your entire being for much more.
Dedicate your heart for a sacred purpose,
Because pain is temporary, but how you endure is the glory;
So continue to craft your hidden love story.

Toni Braxton *"Unbreak My Heart"* (1996) Eve *"Love is Blind"* (1999)
Usher *"My Boo"* (2004) Musiq Soulchild *"Buddy"* (2007)

Insanity
Dedicated to JUW
RIP: MD
(8/2014)

Insanity…
Insanity has this complex plan for you and me,
He poses as a friend,
But works undercover as an enemy.
So, while God keeps lending us
Peace of mind,
That *homie*[6] of mine,
'Insanity' constricts us,
And keeps wasting our time.
When debts add up,
Who collects those fines?
But, "I'm fine";
Because there's money to keep spending,
While my car wheels still spinning;
I couldn't care less if my head's still spinning.

It's probably the shots of tequila
mixed with Patron;
No chasers, baby steps,
What you think--I ain't grown?
Yet, I'm still not growing.

See, this is the secret,
I promised I wouldn't leak it,
But it's far too juicy for me to ever keep it.

'Insanity' is not being 'crazy' —

---

[6] *homie-a close friend, a buddy; acquaintance who has shared a bond or experience.*

That's just a label.
Instead, it's a downhill process where you remain unstable;
Never able
To take the lesson from the mistake;
Playing chances at high stakes.
But, how many risks does it take--
And how many rules can you break,
Before you're able to contemplate
The judgment that wars with your fate?
But
forget all that,
And nix the rest of that;
I mix and count it back.
So tomorrow, it'll be double shots of Patron,
Double shots of tequila;
The night lasts forever,
In the morning I'll chase the painkillers.

But tonight, I'm turning up
Don't worry 'bout what's in my cup.
Because,
You know how I be,
Coked up, smoked out; in the sun, high on that Vitamin D
Only to wake up and wonder 'Damn, who gave me HIV?'
Maybe I lied, I am a tad bit 'crazy'.

Dedicated to MD
Remain in Power JUW

Free Verse

If I needed a cure and you were the anecdote,
Would I remain ill —
Or could you cure me without the use on a single syringe or pill?

                    9 June 2018

Sherrie Elle poetry

Junkie Gene
8/2014, 8/7/2016, 5/18/2017

See, I got this itch that you can't seem to scratch,
And when you see me, my attention you won't be able to grasp.
Thoughts racing,
Mind is pacing;
I can't relapse--
To the aches and the cravings,
So, I spend my last savings
Chasing the next high.
With so many demons to fight--
Who wants lonely days and sleepless night?
So, we daydream through the skylight,
Because if the time is right,
There's always a divine healer.
Some call him the "*plug*[7]";
He just may be a drug dealer.
The only thing I know is that $4 *nick*[8] bag
Saved me at a drop of a dime,
Because all my coins were scraped up until
The next time
I'm paid.
But by then, I upgrade--
So, I need the 'loud' pack;
Two nicks to be exact;
Matter of fact,
"I'll grab an eighth",
But that's just an endless bait.

I graduate

---

[7] *Plug:* slang word for drug dealer, coined by millennials.

[8] *Nick: short for 'nickel', used specifically for $5 small bags of marijuana*

And escalate,
Because 'loud' was only temporary,
He couldn't satisfy me; he failed me.
So tonight, it's Vicodin, Percocet,
Xanex, and codeine;
Mixed with soda, cough syrup--
Some may call it "lean."
All I know is that when I'm on top,
I feel like a sex machine.

So, around and round again;
This elliptical is cyclical,
Cocaine--you can be my new 'best friend',
And then...
Crashing down
On this merry-go 'round,
I dangle to my last rope;
Succumbing to a numbness
Where there's just no hope.
Tiptoeing on pins and needles,
While losing respect from those who always wanted to be like you--
Or like me should I say.
But who am I?
What else do I have to lose?
Is this battle worth the fight;
Which weapon do I choose?
Especially, when there's no job to wake up to in the morning,
No friends or enemies left to do the scorning;
Family--no one cares or give heed to fair warnings.

I'm invisible;
Sort of invincible--because after all,
I've always been so dope.
With the spirit of a heroine,

I wonder why my alter ego and I have never connected?
Finally, I have the courage to commit to the unexpected.
I return to a childhood fear of needles--
Now unafraid of poking and prickings,
And without further thought I stick it in.

Thoughts are racing
Mind is pacing;
This is an unknown memory of no replacement.
My tongue and skin become a shade of blue;
Blank pupils are just an unmarked stare.
I have conquered a journey that reaches far beyond any of my worst nightmares.
No one can hear the screams;
My throat cannot holler or yell--
My body is trapped inside of a cocooned shell;
And now I have finally become a slave in this 8th stage of hell.

Dedicated to suicide survivor UK

Sherrie Elle poetry

Crowns
3/24/2018

She is remarkable--
From the crown of her head,
to the soles of her feet.
Bad--
Commanding attention every time that she speaks.
She dresses fierce,
And her shoe game is only complements of the best.
Competition is a means for those who settle for less.
Because after all, why settle for what she can get,
when she gets what she wants?
But don't fall for the illusion;
It's only a front.

Although she has enough money in the bank,
And the gas in her car never reaches an empty tank;
Her mind is only an Instagram filter,
While her soul remains blank.
But she's bad--
From the crown of her head,
To the soles of her feet;
Rocking the most expensive shoes,
But her inner soul is cheap.
Far beyond school years,
But she hasn't reached any levels or tiers;
Because she's remains unaware
that:
Everything that glitters ain't gold;
And if it's gold, doesn't mean that it won't rust or fade—
Many times, beauty will hide comfortably in the shade.
Please understand this:
A woman is not defined by the shoes she wears on her feet;

It's the footsteps she takes and whether her destiny and
purpose meets.
It's not even about the makeup she wears,
"Slaying[9]" has nothing to do with how she styles her hair.
But does she have enough confidence to make you stop and
stare?
Does her conversation bring you a breath of fresh air?
Is she taking care of her business?
Does she read;
Does she pray?
If her character doesn't motivate you,
Then what role do you expect her to portray?

A woman's crown can never be too heavy,
Because she will always hold the weight on her shoulders,
And it will never slow down her pace;
She walks by having an incredible sense of unspoken grace.
After all, she knows exactly what to do with her income and
first fruits;
You can trust her with your secrets, your time and energy,
because she only knows how to produce.
She puts her hands to beneficial use,
Because it shows forth in her time and investments;
The effect of having her by your side is nothing short of a
blessing.
She is a giver and not a taker,
But don't mistake her
For any one,
Or anybody,
Because if her crown does fall,
It only tilts gently at her feet,

---

[9] *slaying*: used to acknowledge that someone has done something really awesome, has destroyed their competition, looks really sexy or has been very funny.

But she dusts it off and moves forward without any sign of defeat.

Jewel Box
(4/19/2018)

"You're never supposed to get rid of gifts from someone...if it's not your style, leave it as a keepsake."

There was a ring that I adored during my childhood--
It belonged to my oldest Aunty.
It was pure gold--not plated like what is worn today:
Oval shaped, and in the center was a small cubic zirconia--
She had some of the best pendants, clutches and sterling silver
that a person could ever wear.
So, when she gave her oldest niece the ring I've always
admired,
I understood how her level of thinking
was inspired.
Heirlooms are precious items we pass from one generation to
the next.
And it's not about the price, but the sentiment that it leaves
behind.
This is the wealth we keep that surpasses the test of time.

Believe gifts comes from a place warm within the heart.
But feeling your loved one's presence through vibrations
outweighs any souvenir;
Because frequencies of love elevate through the ether and
atmosphere.
But why do we recklessly neglect the most precious gift
given—
Our heart?
It's the most priceless gem we will ever possess,
Yet at times we allow unfruitful people in without a solid
'Yes.'
There's not one thing that a person can buy you,
That increases your net worth or inner value,
Because God is the only one that remains and stands by you.

But a keepsake to always remember:
Gifts granted to you under false pretenses or hidden motives
Are not to be kept;
Freely give those who need them,
Or you'll stow them with personal regret.

Recently I invested in a safe box;
Fully secured,
And double pad locked.
It holds lessons that I'll never disown;
The keys to a secured heart--the most expensive jewel to ever own.

Free Verse

Where there is no justice,
Of course there is no PEACE,
In this world of chaos,
How do we expect senseless violence to CEASE?

Sherrie Elle poetry

2015

Immigrant Mentality
(8/2014, 4/21/2018)

How must we succeed,
When some of the world's children cannot even read--
Because in black neighborhoods their young mothers are obsessed with hair weaves.
Meanwhile, fathers in the home seem to have no need,
And sometimes as a Black I feel I have no need
In this world that looks at me as an outcast.
How can we move on without knowledge of the past?

United we must stand,
But not when one brother has a gun in his hand,
While my grand pop is afraid of where the next stray bullet is going to land.
Technically speaking it's called extermination,
But for some, it's a lack of determination.
Some may call it genocide,
But numbers hardly lie,
So, you can call it death by suicide--
Because who's injecting the drugs in their own veins?
And as a joke, some move strangers in front of moving trains,
And tragically enough, our own mothers are sold crack cocaine;
So, tell me exactly who causes the pain?
We tend to blame those who rape their daughters
By leaving them stripped and insane;
Because after all, *'that's not my little girl.'*
We have no connection to others,
Due to our own small bubbled world.
'But it ain't 'bout nothin' long as I get paid,'
Our ancestors must be doing flips inside of their graves,
Because right now, we don't understand,
Or just don't give a damn,

That they literally worked like slaves and made sacrifices like immigrants
To pave the way for their future leaders and descendants.
'But I ain't worried 'bout nothin' long as my Steph Curry sneakers are the most recent,
I'm just tryna' keep my timepiece flossy and decent.'

But I digress because we've come so far in history and made so much progress,
And yet,
Some of us still don't know who Araminta Ross could possibly be,
Or how many she carried on her back.
You think she gave a damn about hair weave tracks,
While risking lives through those underground railroad tracks?
And why do we get so angry when other ethnic groups come into *'our hood'* and raise businesses in such a short period of time?
But in the bank, we don't got a damn dime,
Or, a savings account;
And won't take the time to teach our young toddlers how to count.
But let me break down the minor difference;
Let's do math--a minus and dividend:
Before natives come to a foreign land,
They keep the youngest child with the eldest--show them the tricks of a trade.
While doing so, they teach them how to preserve;
Instead, we degrade.
And in the same vein,
They maintain good grades.
In fact, they go for honors,
So, when natives cross seas, they quickly outshine us.
They value education because it's not easily awarded to them;

We look down on college because we *"can't afford it."*
But with the spirit of Araminta Ross
That transcends the bloodline of
Jeremiah Hamiltion,
Fannie Lou Hamer,
Ida B. Wells,
As the living springs well of
Michelle Obama,
Oprah Winfrey, and the generations that follow,
May we chase vision and not endless hopes that are shallow.

So if we know the difference between capital and investments,
We'd understand it's the future who we'd invest in.
Because then and only then,
We'd make sacrifices like immigrants to pave the way for our future leaders and descendants,
And then our money wouldn't be borrowed;
We'd actually lend it.

The Body of This Essay
(Prose)
(2014)

I hope these gentle strokes of my pen make your heart skip a beat or flutter.
What if I caressed the inner parts of your soul with every word that I utter?
So—so-so excuse me if I stutter,
I just can't help this spell that you put me under.
And if word symmetry is anything like our body's chemistry,
Then never let this atom split in half,
Because a noun, an adjective, a verb is all that we have--
To keep this sentence in conjunction;
You leave my thoughts in complete dysfunction.
My punctuation
Tends to fluctuate
Every time I'm in your presence.
I'm thankful for every grammatical lesson that you teach me,
Because you reach me
Through every section of the body,
No habla Espanol, but *"toca mi cuerpo"*
And no, I'm not speaking about the contents of a letter or an essay--
More like the role that you play
In my mind's script.
You keep me at your ball point pen's tip.
So, when we scribble inside and out of every line,
We still keep every paragraph perfectly aligned.
On this dotted line, here I sign

Secretly,
Sacredly,
My heart is yours.

Free Verse

If my words alone doesn't make the rhythm of your feet go
PITTER PATTER,
Then I pray the ink bleeds through the pages to
Allow your mind to splatter.

6/2018

Sherrie Elle poetry

<u>Free Verse</u>

Marry the person who keeps you merry,
But until that person comes along,
ALL in ONE remain wholeheartedly in solidarity.

Sherrie Elle poetry

6/19/18

The Bride & Groom
7/2009, 4/18/2018

Standing at the altar seemed to be a figment of my imagination.
The pastor announces *"You may now kiss the bride"*--
But wait, my thoughts collide.
I think back on all the times I lied;
Knowing that once that knot was tied,
I could never leave his side.
We'd eternally be one unto God.

But how could you still want me after all the times I left--
Taking a flight here and there;
Yet faithfully you remained, you always were near.
Nights that I deliberately frustrated you,
Contemplated,
and wanted nothing to do with you.
I left you by the wayside, but you gave me my freedom;
But me, I only came when it was convenient.

Now standing here with you face-to-face,
I feel so ashamed, yet you lift my face
To say,
"All is forgiven, we'll move on from this.
"I know you're not perfect and I don't expect you to be, but we'll work through this thing; I have faith in you and me",
But who am I?
And thinking to myself, "Why?"

It's no way that you'll love me despite all my junk and mess--
Reading my thoughts, you said *"that was a test.*
I knew you would come back,
Because the world couldn't satisfy all the things that you lack.
And,

All those parties and fun times,
Cost you thousands of dollars,
And only pennies were added to your lifetime.
Because when you flirt with death,
I can no longer be lenient,
And when you call for me,
My ears will be deaf,
And you'll be under attack by demons."

My life flashes before my eyes,
The pastor looks at me waiting for my reply.
At this point, I reached an epiphany;
Realizing you truly are God's gift for me.
No longer willing to compromise,
Because being without you, how could I elevate or rise?
"*Yes*", I oblige.
"*Yes* I will accept you with my very life."
Amongst the rejoice, the pastor states,
"You may now kiss the bride."

MasterPeace
(4/6/2018)

I find myself searching for my inner peace,
While battling my outer fears;
Trying to keep the sanity by fighting back the pain and tears.
But,
If life is considered a masterpiece,
Then what's on display?
A collectible item of art, or shriveled clumps of clay?
If my house is considered a masterpiece,
Then how do I master peace,
If there are boxes of clutter and loads of stuff I can't release?
Do I own the property--
Or is someone else's name on the lease?
Some homes only function when there is a war that never cease.
So, build my house brick by brick,
And layer it sturdy,
Because if the foundation isn't strong, then anything stands a chance to hurt me.
And if the rooms are filled with other people's belongings and baggage,
Then I'll toss it all out because I don't need to have it.
No room for unnecessary storage--
Because pack ratting lies, and secrets are only a means of hoarding.
I'll diligently work to construct that masterpiece known as my home,
With limestone, brick, mortar, and hardwood stone,
But understand this, it requires more material than these alone.

If an architect doesn't perfect the craft until he/she completes certain levels of school,
Then how do you expect to master your peace without the proper tools?
And,
If it had taken 9 years to perfect the great painting of Mona Lisa,
And over 25 years to design the Egyptian Sphinx of Giza--
Then what do you believe was the driving force?
Sometimes an artist's legacy is only recognized after their life's course.

So, when my master peace is complete,
Shine the light in every room,
Including the basement;
Because God will remodel--
Starting with the interior,
And ending with those cracks outside the pavement.

Let me remain gentle as a dove and wise as a serpent,
So, He can let in light by removing the blinds and every curtain.
And since no one's backyard is every fully clean,
I can only expect God to remove twigs and branches,
To make His masterpiece pristine.

Because you can master your peace as if it's a hidden castle
Where flowers can easily bloom,
Or a grave stone that only resembles an unmarked tomb.
Can you shine the light in every room in your house--?

If not, then another person name must be on the lease;
Therefore, ask yourself who controls the design to your master peace?

Sphinx of Giza, Cairo

Free Verse

What's your guilty pleasure:
Pasta, seafood, steak,
Or are you a fan of sweets?
There's a fine line between where greed and gluttony
meet.

2018

Legacy
(4/13/2018)

Aunty always said, *"If it was a snake, it would have bit you twice"*,
Because as a child I never watched where I was walking.
"Never let your left hand know what your right is doing",
But so hard-headed, I just kept talking.
And when she said,
"That hard head gon' make a soft behind"
Let there be no more clashes
Or gnashing of teeth,
Because this is a time to turn over a green leaf.
So, if legacy is the only thing that's best for me,
Then what will I leave behind--
A generational barrier
Or a higher rope to climb?
And if my name sake isn't worth much,
Then the future holds more weight;
Because great leaders never begin a journey at an empty slate.
And to some,
I'm not worth a nickel;
Others won't even pay me a dime,
But who cares about the critics of plenty--
Since God smiles on me, let me be a priceless penny.

Free Verse

The limits of boxes won't confine me
Because I am a character that can never be defined.
So at the moment when you think you understand,
Please don't choose me,
Because your predictions will tend to always lose me.
2018

Sherrie Elle poetry

Acknowledgements

First and foremost, I thank the Creator, God, Supreme Being, who may be known by many names. Family, friends and acquaintances in my life to teach, foster, and shape me. Special thanks to Sister Asha Mitchell and Shelley Leaphart-Williams. Jamie Centeno and Virgy Centeno who demonstrates spiritual teachings and wisdom that applies specifically to growth and healing. My college friend, Nate Cottman, who motivated me to move forward in self-publishing with his book entitled *EXECUTE*. Special gratitude to my former professor Dr. Jacqueline Akins for encouraging me in the expertise of English and creative writing by providing necessary resources. It takes a village to raise a person, so therefore *UnCover'd Vol. 1* would not have come into fruition without the mothers, fathers, grandmothers, aunties and other sacred people who continue to uplift and encourage. My birth parents Sherrie Lawyer and Kirk Simmons. Their presence, advice and knowledge cannot be forgotten or ignored.

About the Author

Sherrie Lawyer has been writing creative stories since the age of 7 and poetry before she was 13. Sherrie attended public school in the city of Philadelphia and obtained higher education at the Community College of Philadelphia and Temple University. Sherrie has taken a variety of courses in education, social sciences, child development and counseling. She currently studies world languages and lives abroad.